Electricity and Magnetism

Predominant artwork & imagery source: Shutterstock.com

Copyright: North Parade Publishing Ltd.

4 North Parade,

Bath,

BA1 1LF, UK

This edition ©2021

All rights reserved. No part of this publication may be reprinted, stored in a retrieval system or transmitted, in any form or by any means, electronic, mechanical, photocopying, recording, or otherwise, without the prior permission of the copyright holder.

Printed in China.

Contents

INTRODUCTION TO ELECTRICITY 6
STATIC ELECTRICITY 8
ELECTRICAL CURRENT 12
CONDUCTORS AND INSULATORS 14
ELECTRIC FIELD 16
DIRECT CURRENT AND ALTERNATING CURRENT 18
ELECTRONICS 20
ELECTRONIC COMPONENTS 22
GENERATION OF ELECTRICITY 24
ELECTRIC CIRCUITS 26
ELECTRICAL APPLIANCES 28
MAGNETISM 30
MAGNETIC FIELD 32
MAGNETIC MATERIALS 34
MAGNETIC LEVITATION 36
ELECTROMAGNETIC RADIATION 38
ELECTROMAGNETISM 40
ELECTROMAGNETS 42
APPLICATIONS OF ELECTROMAGNETISM AND EM RADIATION 44

Introduction to Electricity

Electricity is associated with stationary or flowing electrons. The word 'electricity' is derived from the Greek word 'elektron' which means 'amber.' We use electricity to power household objects and also to run massive factories and machines. Electricity is generated from different sources to meet the demands of houses, public resources and industry.

Nature of Electricity

All matter around us is made up of atoms. The atom has a nucleus with protons and neutrons and electrons revolve around the nucleus. The nucleus has a net positive charge (protons are positively charged and neutrons do not have any charge). The electrons are negatively charged. The electrons and the nucleus attract each other due to their opposite charges.

If the electrons are able to move from one atom to another, then that material is capable of conducting electricity. Normally, the electrons move randomly and irregularly across the atoms in every direction, so there is no net movement of charge and no flow of electrons. When all electrons move or flow together in one direction, it creates an electric current.

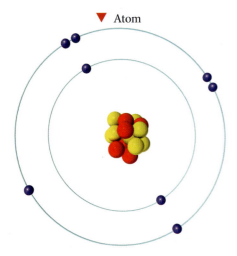
▼ Atom

▼ Lightning

Understanding Electricity: A Brief History

Long before people understood electricity, they observed and marveled at the power of lightning and how it could sometimes strike something. The ancient people of different civilisations were also aware of species of fish and sting rays that were capable of inducing electric shocks.

In 600 BC, Thales of Miletus, a Greek philosopher, discovered the phenomenon of static electricity when he rubbed fur and amber and used the amber to pick up small scraps and dust.

William Gilbert, who discovered the science of magnetism, was also responsible for using the term 'electricus' that later gave rise to the term 'electricity.' Later, in the 18th century, Benjamin Franklin conducted experiments in electricity, the most famous among them being the one in which he used a kite and a key during a lightning storm to prove that lightning was electrical in nature.

Many others played an important role in understanding electricity and enabling its use. Alessandro Volta invented the electrical battery. Michael Faraday studied electricity extensively and also developed the electric motor. Thomas Edison and Nikola Tesla also made important contributions in the field of electricity. While Edison is credited for the invention of the light bulb, Tesla invented the alternating current (AC) system that is used extensively today.

▲ Benjamin Franklin

▲ Michael Faraday

Types of Electricity

Static electricity and current electricity are the two types.

Static electricity: It is caused by the buildup of electric charges (positive or negative) on the surface of certain materials. This kind of electricity is produced due to friction or contact. The effects of static electricity are observed as sparks, shocks, or clinging of materials.

Current Electricity: It is a form of electricity produced when electrons flow in one direction inside a conducting material.

▲ Electric lines

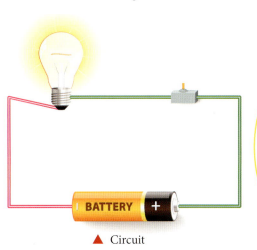
▲ Circuit

FUN FACT

When the switch is flipped on, the electrons in the wire flow at nearly the speed of light, which is 3×10^8 metres/second!

7

Static Electricity

Static electricity is produced due to the buildup of electric charges on the surface of certain materials. When the materials are rubbed together or pulled apart, one material acquires a positive charge and the other acquires a negative charge, and the resulting imbalance produces static electricity in observable forms.

Static Electricity

Static electricity is so named to differentiate it from current electricity, where electrons flow. Two materials are involved in the generation of static electricity. One of these materials has an excess of electrons, or a negative charge. Another material that has lost electrons gains a positive charge. When these two materials interact by rubbing together, electrons are pulled from the surface of one material onto another. This effect is known as 'triboelectric charging.'

Static Electricity in Nature

In nature, static electricity is formed under different conditions. Usually, low humidity and dry air is ideal for generation of static electricity. When the air is humid or carries a lot of water vapour, the water molecules can collect on the materials and prevent the buildup of electrical charges.

However, extreme turbulence in the air caused by a thunderstorm cloud can result in static charge generation as the water drops down from the clouds. Benjamin Franklin performed a dangerous experiment by flying a kite with a metal key string attached to it during a storm. The static electricity caused an electric spark in the key.

◀ Hair standing up due to static electricity

Effects of Static Electricity

Static electricity causes any of the following effects:

Attraction: When a balloon is vigorously rubbed on a wool sweater, the balloon acquires a negative charge on its surface while the wool acquires a positive charge. The balloon can then be made to stick temporarily to the wall, which does not have an excess of either positive or negative charge. The same effect is observed when you comb your hair and use the comb to attract small shreds of paper.

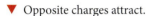
▼ Opposite charges attract.

▲ Balloon and paper attraction

Repulsion: When you use a plastic comb on dry hair, the comb acquires negative charges in the process. The strands of hair, left with an excess of positive charges, will repel each other, resulting in them sticking up for a few seconds.

Sparks: Sparks are produced under circumstances when there are enough positive charges on one material and negative charges on another material. In such a case, the attraction between the positive and negative charges is so great that it makes electrons jump the air gap between the two objects. Such jumping electrons heat up the air and this, in turn, causes more electrons to jump across the gap. When the air gets hot enough, it glows briefly, resulting in a spark.

FUN FACT

Lightning is an example of a powerful form of static electricity. The temperature of a lightning bolt can reach 28,000°C.

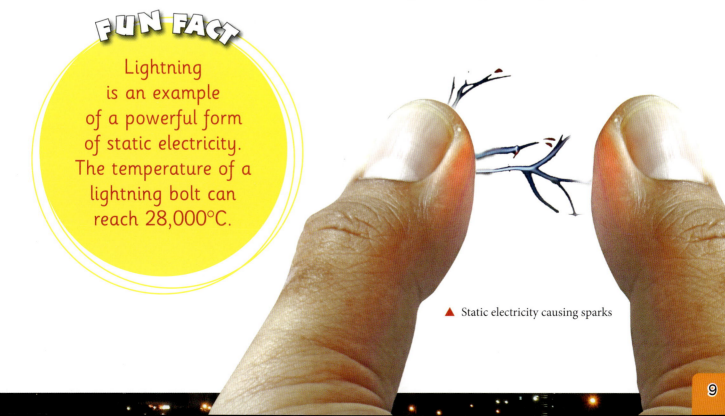
▲ Static electricity causing sparks

Static Electricity

There are many methods to artificially produce static electricity by using suitable materials. Static electricity can also be generated in specially designed devices for research and demonstration. Static electricity can be harnessed and employed for different purposes.

Static Electricity Devices

Electroscope: This is one of the first known electrical measuring instruments. It was invented by William Gilbert around 1600. The electroscope is used for roughly measuring the presence and magnitude of electric charge. The device detects the electric charge of an object through its movement. However, this device is only useful for measuring more than hundreds of thousands of volts.

▲ Electroscope

Electrophorus: This device was invented by a Swedish scientist, Johan Carl Wilcke, in 1764 and later its design was improved by Alessandro Volta. It combines the creation of static electricity along with electrostatic induction to charge a metal plate repeatedly. Static electricity charges are induced on the plate by rubbing with wool or fur. The plate develops negative charge. When a metal plate is then brought into contact, the two plates attract. When the plates are pulled apart, the charges are transferred onto the metal plate and can be used for producing sparks for demonstrating static electricity.

▲ Electrophorus

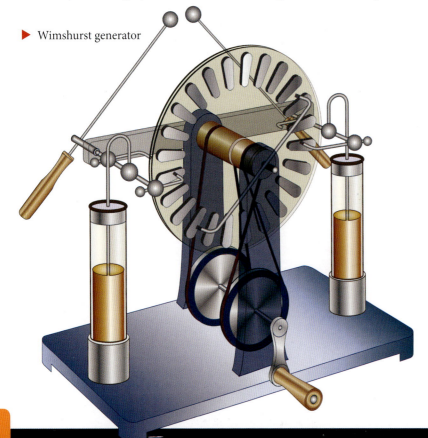

▶ Wimshurst generator

Wimshurst generator: Modern versions of Wimshurst generators—originally invented in the 1880s—consist of two plastic discs that rotate in opposite directions through a crank or belt-driven mechanism. As the discs turn, the metal foil sectors get charged and the accumulated charges are transmitted to a storage capacitor. This generator can produce up to 75,000 volts. Despite the high voltage, the current is low enough so that it isn't dangerous. This generator is used for producing sparks and conducting static electricity experiments.

Van de Graaff generator: This generator is powered by a high-speed electric motor and consists of two pulleys and a belt running along it. The lower pulley is an insulating material, while the upper pulley is made of metal. The high speed of the belt movement and buildup of a massive amount of charge enables it to produce great voltages of about 400,000 volts. Large generators can produce sparks that can travel across a room.

Uses of Static Electricity

It might be easy to assume that static electricity is mostly useful only for the purpose of studying and demonstration. But static electricity has a few other practical uses too:

Painting cars: Automobile manufacturers employ static electricity for painting cars. The car's surface is first prepared for painting and placed in a painting booth. Specially designed, electrically charged paint is sprayed as a fine mist into the booth. The charged particles get attracted to the car's surface and stick to the body evenly and are distributed smoothly after drying, which cannot be achieved by manual painting.

Photocopying documents: A standard photocopier machine works on the principle of static electricity to make copies of documents. Electrically charged ink is used for specifically sticking to certain places on the paper.

Pollution control: Devices that can collect charged dirt particles in the air onto a plate with opposite charge are used for clearing a space of dirt and dust. This type of device is known as an electrostatic precipitator.

Smokestack: In factories that produce smoke, static electricity is used to reduce air pollution. The smoke is electrically charged so that it clings to electrodes of the opposite charge, which are placed in the smokestacks instead of being released into the air.

Air fresheners: Air fresheners work on a principle similar to the pollution control in smokestacks. The devices are capable of removing electrons from smoke, dust, and pollen, and the positively charged particles are then attracted to a negatively charged plate in the air freshener, resulting in cleaner air.

◀ Van de Graaff generator

FUN FACT

The Van de Graaff generator, despite producing high voltages, generates only enough electric current needed to light up a 4-watt bulb.

◀ Photocopier

Electrical Current

The movement of electrical energy from one place to another so that it can be utilised for powering devices is called current. An electric current is produced by the motion of electrons in a suitable conducting material.

Electric Current and Voltage

The movement of charged particles (electrons), from one section to another, produces an electric current. The electrons are in motion along a specific path, which may be a conducting material like copper, aluminium or silver.

The electric current depends on the rate at which the electric charge flows through the conductor. A pump can be used to force water to flow quicker through a pipe. Similarly, using an external source of power such as a battery can push free electrons faster through the conductor in a specific path. If more electrons pass a given point in a second, the current is said to be greater. Current is measured in amperes.

Voltage is a measure of the difference in electrical potential between two points in an electric circuit. It is measured in volts.

▲ Electric wires

FUN FACT

A bird sitting on a power line is safe as long as it does not touch another line with its wing or leg. When it does so, a circuit is produced and causes electrocution.

◀ Bird on a power line

Resistance

Any force that opposes the motion of the electrons in a conducting wire is known as resistance. If a thin wire is used, the electrons do not have enough space to flow smoothly, and in this case the wire is said to have high resistance. In contrast, a thick wire provides more space for the movement of electrons and has lower resistance. Resistance is measured in ohms.

In simple terms, resistance refers to any obstruction in the way of electricity. If you think of an electric circuit with a light bulb in between, the bulb is a source of resistance. The obstacle uses up some of the electricity flowing through the circuit.

Uses of Electricial Current

Electrical devices: Morse code and the telegraph were invented using long-distance transmission through electricity.

Light sources: The first use of electricity for homes was for lighting. Light bulbs were followed by better and improved lights and lamps.

Batteries: Batteries are capable of converting chemical energy into electrical energy and are used for powering video games, remote-controlled toys, flashlights, and other small devices.

▲ Electric bulb

Motors: Motors are used for powering many appliances including power tools, water pumps, vehicles and industrial machines. A motor converts electrical energy into mechanical energy.

Medical uses: Many machines used in diagnosis and treatment of patients require electricity. A few examples of medical diagnosis devices include electrocardiograms, X-ray machines, scanning devices, and ventilation systems.

▲ Motor

Generators: All modern establishments like hospitals, schools, colleges, workplaces, factories and shops use generators as backup when the power supply fails. A generator can store electrical energy for later use.

▶ Electric generator

Conductors and Insulators

Materials are classified as conductors or insulators based on their ability to conduct electricity. Both conductors and insulators are useful, and often both are used together, as in the case of wires for combining utility and safety.

Conductors

▶ Copper wires

Conductors are those materials that permit electrons to move freely from atom to atom. A conducting material will allow electric charge to distribute across its entire surface, when charge is transferred to a certain location. The distribution of charge happens due to movement of electrons. When the conductor is touched by another conductor, the charge can be transferred through the free movement of electrons. Materials that are capable of high conductivity are referred to as superconductors.

Examples of conductors include metals such as iron, silver, aluminium, and copper; their alloys, such as brass and bronze; ionic salts dissolved in water; graphite; and the human body.

▲ Conducting materials

The Van de Graaff generator is useful for proving that the human body is conductive to electric charge. When a person touches the static ball of the generator, the excessive charge on the ball is transferred to the person and spreads everywhere, including the hair. When all the hair strands acquire the same charge, they repel each other and stand straight up.

Charge Distribution

It is possible to predict the direction in which the electrons move in a conducting material by applying two rules of charge interaction: 1) Opposite charges attract; 2) Like charges repel.

If a conductor imparts a net negative charge at one location, there is an excess of electrons in that spot. Since the electrons all possess the same negative charge, they repel each other and try to move away or distance themselves. These electrons then begin to migrate on the conductor, distributing evenly across the surface.

When the conductor is instead given a positive charge by removing electrons, there is an excess of protons instead, but the same two rules of charge interaction apply. Since protons are bound to the nucleus and are not capable of movement, the electrons will help distribute the charge evenly across the surface. Electrons that are loosely bound to their atoms leave and move over to other atoms. The electron migration continues until the overall repulsion effect is minimised.

Insulators

Insulators are materials that impede the free flow of electrons between atoms. If electric charge is transferred to an insulator, the excess charge will remain in the location of transfer and will not be distributed across its surface, as free movement of electrons does not occur. Rubber, plastic, ceramic, glass, Styrofoam, paper, and dry air are examples of insulators.

▲ Plastic   ▲ Rubber   ▲ Ceramic

Increasing Conducting Ability →

Insulators	Semi-conductors	Conductors
Rubber, Glass, Wood, Dry Air	Silicon, Germanium, Water, Mercury	Carbon, Iron, Aluminium, Copper, Silver

Uses of Conductors and Insulators

Conductors are used for transferring electric charge in the form of objects and wires. Owing to their conducting nature, conductors are mounted on top of or surrounded by an insulator material for safety. Household appliances have copper wires enclosed in plastic or rubber coating to avoid electric shock. Experiments are often performed using conductors mounted on insulators to enable them to be manipulated safely.

▼ Conductor and insulator

FUN FACT

A metal conductor may be up to 10^{18} (a million trillion) times more conductive than glass!

Electric Field

An electric field is an area that can influence charge within a circuit as the charge travels from one location to another. The electric force, like gravity, is a noncontact force that can influence without having to be directly in contact.

Electric Charge

Only charged particles exhibit an electric field. If the electrically charged particles are also moving, they generate a magnetic field. The combined electric and magnetic field is referred to as the electromagnetic field. Electric charge is the physical property of any particle to experience a force when placed in an electromagnetic field.

The electric charge can be either positive or negative. Any material which has no net charge is called neutral. Substances that have more protons than electrons have a positive charge, while those with more electrons than protons possess a negative charge.

Any object's total electric charge is calculated as the sum of the electrical charges of all the particles that make up the object. Usually, electric charge is small and insignificant because objects are made up of atoms that usually have the same number of electrons (negative charge) and protons (positive charge).

Electric Field

A single electric charge will attract or repel another charge brought close to it. This ability to attract or repel is stored in a certain region around the electric charge. This region is referred to as the electric field. All charged particles have electric fields around them.

A Van de Graaff generator is a good example of a charged object that generates an electric field. The field is so intense that without even having to touch the static ball, you can experience a strange sensation just as you pass by.

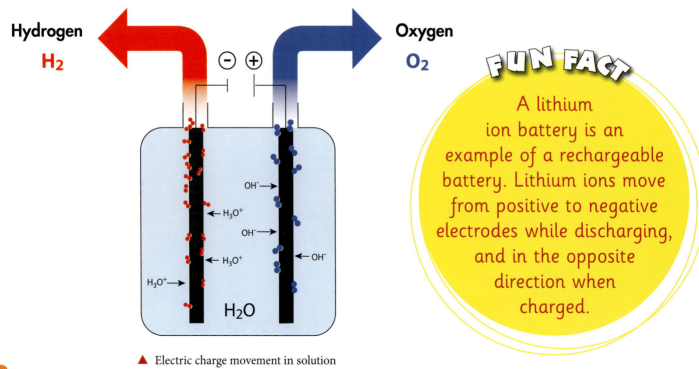

▲ Electric charge movement in solution

FUN FACT

A lithium ion battery is an example of a rechargeable battery. Lithium ions move from positive to negative electrodes while discharging, and in the opposite direction when charged.

Lines of Force

An electric field can be visualised as imaginary lines known as the 'lines of force.' Even though the lines of force are imaginary, it is helpful for visualising the electric field. This field of force can exert its effect without direct physical contact. Any charged object when brought close to the electric field will alter the field in a certain way. The more a charged object moves into a field, the more pronounced and noticeable the effect.

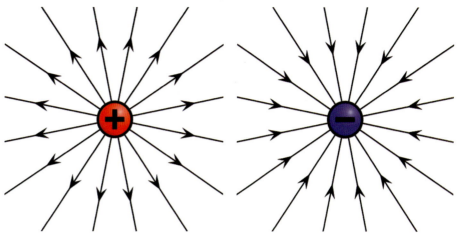

▲ Lines of force

Electric lines of force can indicate the direction in which a positive or negative charge would move in the presence of another charge. The lines of force around a positively charged object radiate in all directions away from the object. The lines around a negatively charged object radiate toward the object.

When another object of opposite charge is brought close, the lines of force will connect. When similarly charged objects are brought close to each other, the lines of force will never connect. In order to move a charge in an electric field away from its natural direction, you must exert a specific external force.

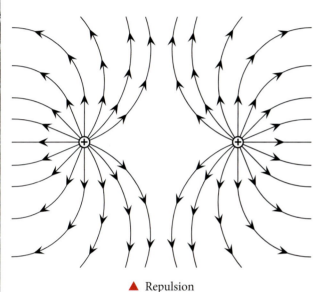

▲ Repulsion

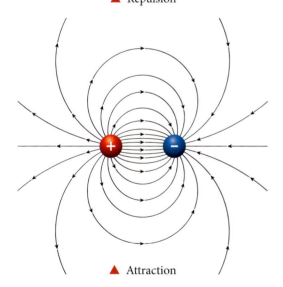

▲ Attraction

Nature of Electric Force

The electric force is the fundamental factor that keeps the electrons bound to the nucleus of an atom. It is this force that is responsible for chemical bonding between elements to produce molecules.

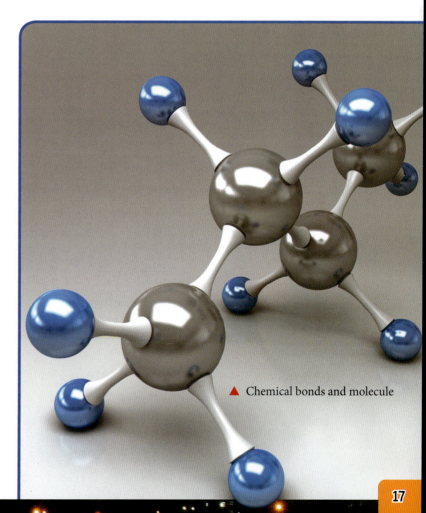

▲ Chemical bonds and molecule

Direct Current and Alternating Current

There are two main types of current: direct current (DC) and alternating current (AC). They differ mainly in the direction in which the electric current flows. Both these types of current serve useful purposes depending on the need.

Direct Current

In Direct Current, the current flow is in a single direction and does not change periodically. Direct current is used for powering electrical devices and charging batteries. Fuel cells, solar cells, and batteries produce direct current. Electric vehicles, mobile phone batteries, flashlights, and flat-screen televisions use direct current. DC is represented as a straight line.

▶ Batteries

▶ Solar cells

In direct current, the electrons move slowly but continuously in one direction and travel from one end to the other. The voltage is also constant or almost constant. If you take a 1.5-volt battery, the voltage it provides will always be 1.5 volts. Similarly, the positive terminal will always remain the positive terminal, and the same holds true for the negative terminal. As a result, the electrons will move only in one direction.

FUN FACT

Michael Faraday tested alternating current for the first time in 1832 using his dynamo electric generator.

Alternating Current

As the name suggests, alternating current (AC) keeps switching directions forward and backward periodically. It is the most commonly used type of current, and is preferred for powering household electrical appliances as well as for businesses. It is represented as a curved line wave form known as a sine wave. The waves or the curved lines represent the alternating current's cycles, which are measured in hertz.

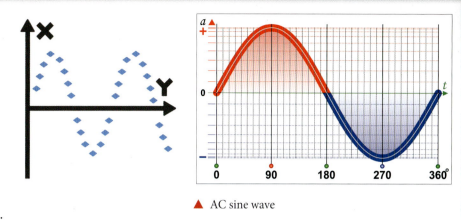

▲ AC sine wave

The voltage in alternating current periodically reverses itself, and every time this happens, the direction of the current flow changes. In power distribution systems across the world, the voltage is reversed about 50 to 60 times per second. The electrons do not move in a flow but instead wiggle back and forth—that is, they move in one direction, turn around, and move in the opposite direction so that the net effect is that they haven't moved.

The reason why alternating current is the preferred one for transmitting across long distances, is its efficiency. Direct current loses more power than alternating current when it flows for long distances.

The mechanism of Newton's cradle explains how alternating current works. The device consists of a wooden frame with a series of metal balls hung in such a way that they are in a line and touching each other. If a ball at one end is pulled and released, it swings forward to propel the ball on the other end to swing, which in turn strikes back. The alternating motion can continue for a long time before the balls come to rest.

The electrons in AC move in one direction and then reverse and move in the opposite direction back and forth as long as the voltage reverses continuously. The voltage constantly changes from the maximum positive to zero and then to the maximum negative, then back to zero and so on in cycles.

In a power grid, a transformer is used for converting AC to high voltages (about 1 million volts) to make it easier to transmit across a long distance and then drop it back down to lower voltages for distribution to houses.

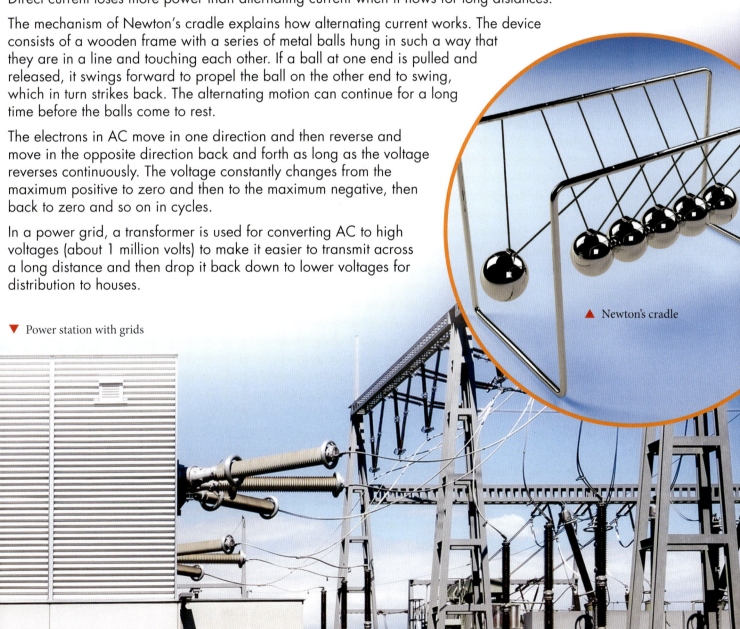

▼ Power station with grids

▲ Newton's cradle

Electronics

Today, electronics are used everywhere, for functions ranging from storing money to guiding airplanes to monitoring your heartbeat. The science of electronics deals with manipulating electrons to control operations and process information. Electronics has enabled the development of computer technology and robotics.

▼ Electronic circuit

Difference between Electricity and Electronics

Electricity deals with making electrons flow around a circuit to drive a motor or an appliance. Generally, these electrical devices require a lot of energy to enable their function and deal with high levels of electric currents. Electronics, on the other hand, use tiny electric currents to power components. In theory, single electrons are carefully navigated around complex circuits to process signals. To give a comparison, if an electric kettle operates on a current of 10 amperes, an electronic component would use only a fraction of a milliampere.

Analog and Digital Signals

Electronic equipment can store data in analog or digital form. Radios used to be designed with antennae to catch radio waves transmitted from a radio station. The waves vibrate up and down in a pattern corresponding to the voices or music, and these signals are converted into sounds that can be heard. This is an example of analog signals. A modern radio works differently. The signals are received in the digital format as coded numbers and then converted into sounds.

Digital electronics dominate all types of modern electronic equipment such as smartphones, hearing aids, cameras, computers and tablets.

▼ Electronic devices

Electronic Circuits

An electronic device's function is decided not just by the components within it but also in the way those components are arranged in circuits. The simplest circuit is a continuous loop connecting two components, while a complicated circuit can have different circuit connections between more than two components.

Generally, analog appliances have simpler electronic circuits than digital appliances. For instance, a transistor radio will have a few components and a circuit board about the size of a book. On the other hand, a computer will have complex circuits with millions of separate pathways. A complex circuit can perform more intricate operations than a simple one.

Circuit Board

In the laboratory, a simple circuit can be assembled by connecting electronic components with the help of short lengths of copper cables. However, when one uses many components, it becomes difficult to connect them. To address this problem, components are arranged and assembled in a systematic way on a circuit board.

A circuit board is a rectangular piece of plastic with copper connecting tracks on one surface and holes drilled through it for connecting components by poking them through the holes and using the copper tracks to link them together or cutting off excess bits when necessary. Extra wires can also be added for making additional connections. This basic type of circuit board is also simply referred to as 'bread board.'

In electronic equipment, instead of these hand-assembled bread boards, factory-made plastic circuit boards with the circuit chemically printed on the surface are used. The copper tracks are also automatically created in a mass manufacturing facility. They are then pushed through pre-drilled holes and fastened into place. They are known as printed circuit boards (PCBs).

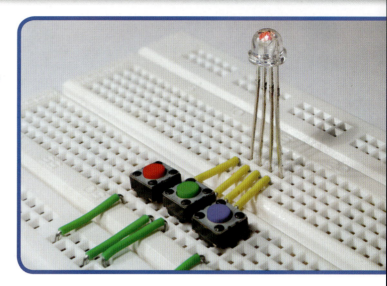

▲ Bread board

Microchips

It was the invention of microchips that created a revolution in the field of information technology. Miniature forms of electronic components were called integrated circuits. It is possible to squeeze millions of miniature components onto a chip no bigger than a person's fingernail. This also made it possible to make sleeker and faster computers and laptops.

▲ Microchip

FUN FACT

Electronic components are held in place with the help of an electrically conductive sticky material called solder.

Electronic Components

Electronic equipment is made up of many tiny components that perform different functions and are linked together through cables or metal connectors. These components are built from a small number of standard parts. These parts can be put together in different places to enable unique functions.

Despite their differences, electronic components have one factor in common. No matter what function they perform, the flow of electrons needs to be controlled in a very specific way. Also, all the solid components are made up of part-conducting and part-insulating materials. The combination of conducting and insulating materials in one component is also known as a semiconductor.

Some of the common electronic parts include:

Resistors: These are the simplest and most basic components of any electronic circuit. The main job of a resistor is to restrict the flow of electrons and thus control the flow of current flowing through the circuit. This is accomplished by converting electrical energy into heat. Resistors are available in different sizes.

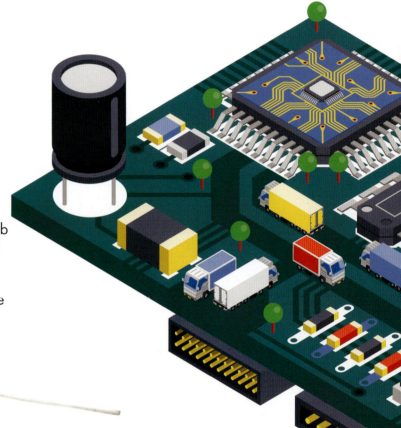

▲ Resistor

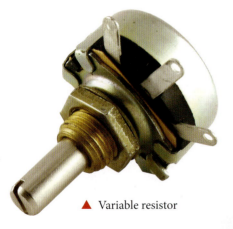

▲ Variable resistor

Capacitors: A capacitor is a simple component made up of two pieces of conducting material, usually made of metal, called 'plates' and separated by an insulating material called dielectric.' Capacitors can store electrical energy just like a battery. When a capacitor is recharged with energy, it is called 'charging' and when it releases energy it is said to be 'discharging.' The amount of electrical energy that a capacitor can store is known as 'capacitance.' They are most often used in timing devices. It is also useful as a tuning device in televisions and radios.

▶ Capacitor

Transistors: A transistor is a miniature electronic component made of silicon that can act as an amplifier or a switch. A transistor can take a small amount of electric current at one end and produce a much bigger output current through amplification. Hence, transistors are useful in hearing aids.

Since transistors can also function as switches, they are the major component of memory chips. Transistors that are connected together make devices that are called logic gates. These logic gates are useful in yes/no decision-making. A typical chip will have billions of transistors capable of being switched on or off.

▲ Transistor

Diodes: A diode is an electronic component that allows current to flow through it in only one direction. Diodes are also known as rectifiers. Diodes are useful in converting alternating current to direct current. Diodes resemble a resistor but work differently. While a resistor can be inserted either way in a circuit board, a diode can be inserted only in a specific direction.

▲ Diode

Optical electronic components: A photoelectric cell is a type of electronic component that can produce tiny electric currents when light falls on it. In contrast, a light-emitting diode (LED) works in the opposite way by emitting light when it receives tiny electric currents.

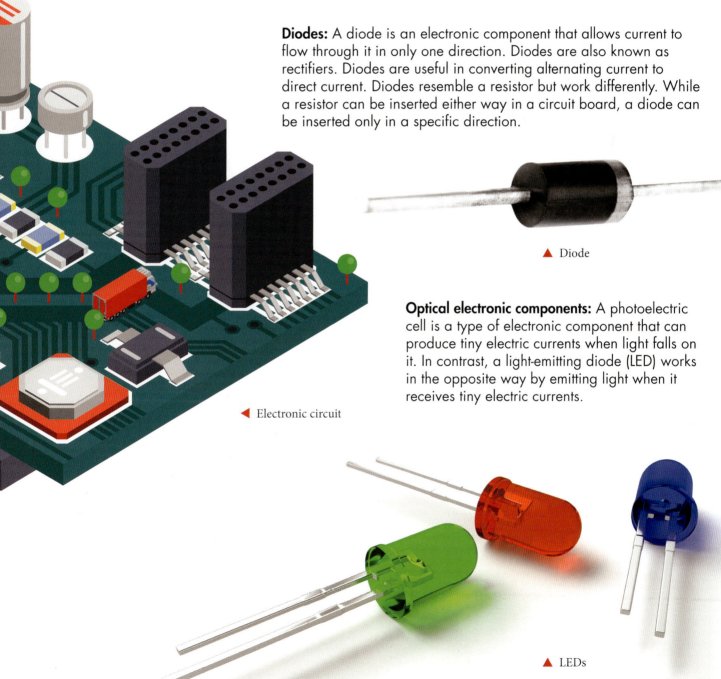

◀ Electronic circuit

▲ LEDs

Generation of Electricity

Electricity is necessary for the household, public, and industrial needs of people across the world. There are different ways to generate electricity, some of which are efficient or nonpolluting while others are inefficient or pollute the environment.

Electric Power Plants

Electric power plants use steam, water, wind, or gas combustion turbines to drive generators. An electricity generator is a device that converts the movement of magnetism inside a coil of wire into electric current. Generators operate on the basis of the relation between electricity and magnetism. The generator is equipped with insulated coils of wire and a rotating electromagnetic shaft. The combined currents produced in each coil add up to one large current that moves from the generator to the power lines and to the buildings.

Fossil Fuels

The dead and buried remains of plants and animals that lived millions of years ago gave rise to fossil fuels like coal, natural gas and petroleum. Burning fossil fuels is a major source of electricity. However, burning fossil fuels can produce pollution and release of carbon dioxide. Fossil fuels are nonrenewable resources and will not last for long.

◀ Fossil fuels

Thermal Power Plants

Thermal power plants use heat to generate electricity. Water is heated until it turns into steam of high temperature. When this steam is channeled through a turbine, it causes the blades in the shaft to spin, and when this rotor is connected to a generator, the movement is converted into electricity.

FUN FACT
Currently, fossil fuels contribute to about 85 percent of the energy consumed across the world.

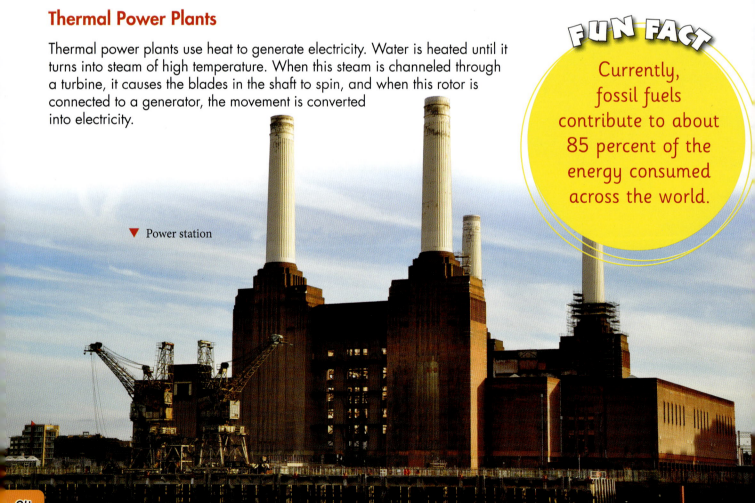
▼ Power station

Nuclear Power

Nuclear plants and power stations generate electricity through steam generated from the heat produced by the atomic fission of radioactive elements like uranium and plutonium. Nuclear plants do not require massive amounts of fuel as in the case of fossil fuels. However, the many safety, health, and environmental hazards associated with the elements used make nuclear power controversial.

▲ Hydroelectric plant

Hydroelectric Plants

Hydroelectricity can be harvested from fast-moving currents in suitable water bodies or reservoirs with dams. Pumped storage is a type of hydroelectricity generated from water pumped through a turbine to generate electricity during periods of low water demand.

▲ Wind turbines

Geothermal Plants

Erupting geysers are a natural source of steam that can be used for generating electricity with very low levels of pollution. The thermal energy harvested from geothermal plants is used for electricity generation as well as heating purposes.

Wind Power

Wind power is generated from the motion of windmills and causes no pollution. However, wind energy is not as effective as water in generating electricity. The most effective way to harness wind power is to use a few large windmills or several small windmills. Only certain locations on the planet are suitable for generating wind power.

Fuel Cells

Fuel cells combine chemical substances to generate electricity through a continuous flow of fuel. Space shuttles are often powered by fuel cells that combine hydrogen and oxygen continuously to generate electricity and water. Fuel cells are not suitable for large installations providing mass power supply because they are difficult to make and operate.

Solar Power

Solar cells, also known as photovoltaic cells, consist of a series of cells wired together and capable of producing electricity when sunlight strikes them. Solar power is nonpolluting and the Sun is a continuous source of fuel. Even though not all the sunlight that strikes the panels is converted into electricity, and they are expensive, solar power is still an attractive option for harnessing sunlight.

▼ Solar panels

Electric Circuits

A circuit is a closed loop that provides a path for the electrons to flow continuously. A voltage is required to make the electrons move from a region of lower potential energy to a region of higher potential energy.

Basics of a Circuit

A simple circuit can be built using a battery with a positive and negative terminal. The positive terminal has an excess of positive charges and the negative terminal has an excess of negative charges. This creates a potential difference that will allow electrons to flow when a conducting wire is connected between the two terminals.

When a wire is connected directly to the two ends of a battery, it produces a lot of energy that is converted into heat and can even destroy the wire. Instead, the electrical energy can be used to power something. When a light bulb, for instance, is placed between the wires, it becomes a functional circuit.

A load is something we place in a circuit that can make use of the electricity generated and convert it into something else, like light or sound.

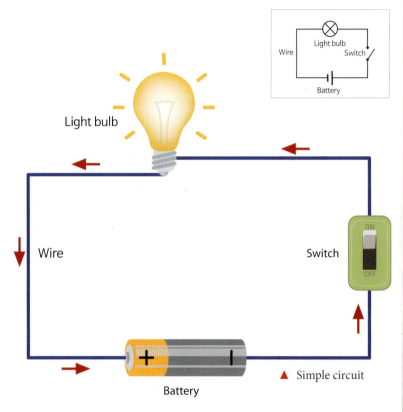

▲ Simple circuit

Short Circuit

When a wire is connected directly from the positive to negative side of a power supply, it can lead to a short circuit. If there is a load connected in the circuit, the flow of current will be limited to the device. However, if there's no load connected, the current will not be slowed down and it will try to flow indefinitely.

The power supply cannot provide infinite current, but it will provide the maximum supply possible and lead to a wire heating up, burning, and damaging the power supply.

▲ Short Circuit

Open Circuit

An open circuit is the opposite of a short circuit, in that the loop isn't fully connected. In other words, it isn't considered as a circuit. This circuit will not work until the broken connection or loose wire is fixed.

Parallel and Series Circuits

Electrical and electronic circuits can be connected in parallel or in series.

A parallel circuit consists of components that are connected along multiple paths so that the same voltage is applied to each component in it. In this circuit, the voltage remains constant while the total current in the circuit is equal to the sum of currents passing through each component.

A series circuit has components that are connected along a single path so that the current that flows through all the components is the same and the voltage across the circuit is equal to the sum of voltages applied to each component.

For example, when a battery is connected to four bulbs, joining one bulb after another in a continuous loop, it is said to be a series circuit. If, instead, each bulb is connected to the battery in a separate loop, then it is a parallel circuit.

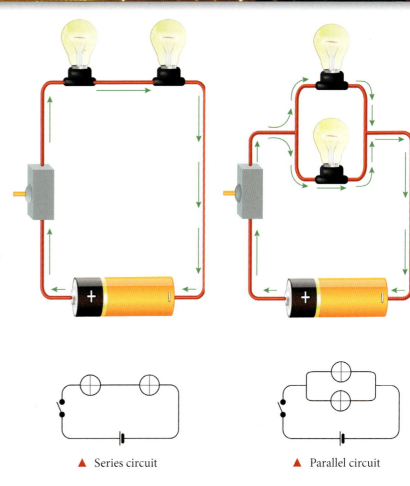

▲ Series circuit ▲ Parallel circuit

FUN FACT

In a series circuit, all the components connected must function so that it is a complete circuit. Even if one component stops working, it will break the entire circuit.

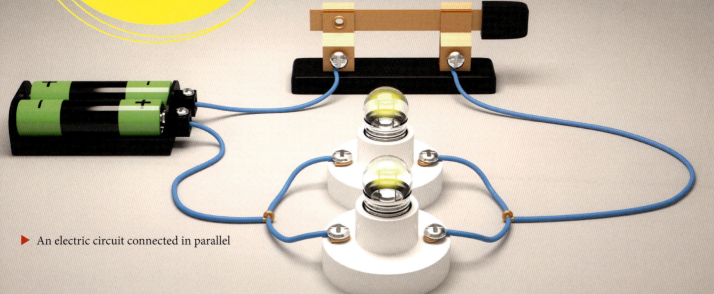

▶ An electric circuit connected in parallel

Electrical Appliances

We use electricity every day to power all our appliances and it comes from electrons moving in sync to produce heat, light or movement. Electricity and magnetism work together as electromagnetism for making electrical appliances work.

▲ Fan

All-purpose Motors

One thing common to all electrical appliances is that they are powered by electricity either in the form of batteries or direct plug-in power supplies through wall-mounted sockets. Apart from this, most of the appliances work by powering an electric motor. A motor is a device equipped with wire endings, magnets, and a rotating shaft.

The electrons in the wire begin to get organised and make the motor spin by turning the wire into an electromagnet. The magnets around the electromagnet are set up in such a way that the attractive and repulsive forces give rise to constant spinning motion in the electromagnet. When the motor receives electricity and converts it into rotational energy, this rotational energy can power a wide range of mechanical work.

Fans, washing machines, and other similar appliances work through the spinning motion of wheels or blades. This spinning motion is powered by motors that rotate when connected to a power supply. Food processors and blenders work in a similar way. They are powered by rotating blades attached to the motor's shaft.

Vacuum cleaners also use a motor to convert electrical energy to mechanical energy. In this appliance, the rotating device creates suction to pull in dirt and dust and will have an air intake, filter and outlet.

▲ Washing machine

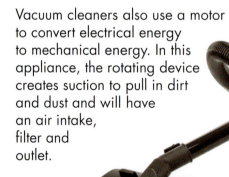
▲ Vacuum cleaner

▲ Disassembled motor

Heating Appliances

When current passes through wire, it naturally heats up a little. This is because of the movement of electrons as they bombard the metal atoms. The energy of the movement is given out as heat. Copper wires are generally used when there is a need for electrons to move around easily without expending too much energy as heat.

However, in appliances that need to produce heat, such as a blow dryer or toaster, wires are instead made of a nickel and chromium alloy called nichrome. When electrons pass through this alloy, they produce a lot of heat. At the atomic level, this is because the electrons often bump into nickel and chromium atoms (more frequently than in copper) and leak heat constantly.

▲ Toaster

Generators

A generator is almost the reverse of an electric motor. A motor receives electricity as the input and provides rotational energy or mechanical energy as the output. A generator uses any other source to produce rotation, and electrical energy is the output. A gas-powered generator has a gasoline engine that can make a shaft turn, and this movement is converted into electricity.

A dynamo is a type of generator that converts the mechanical energy expended in pedaling into electricity to power the electric lamp. A small windmill is equipped with a generator that can convert the motion of the blades into electricity.

▲ Generator

Safety

Since electric currents can be dangerous, appliances must be handled with care. Those that repeatedly blow a fuse must be repaired or replaced. Frays or cracks in electric cords must be replaced. No power outlet should be overloaded with too many appliances at the same time. Water and electricity should never mix—keep electric appliances away from water sources, and no switch or plug should be handled with wet hands.

FUN FACT

Direct current is used in cordless appliances like trimmers whereas a typical wall power outlet works on alternating current.

▲ Safe handling of electrical appliances

Magnetism

Magnetism is a physical phenomenon exhibited by certain materials that make them capable of producing a magnetic field and attracting or repelling other similar substances.

▲ Types of Magnets

▲ Compass

▲ Magnetite (Lodestone)

Understanding Magnetism: History

Magnetic materials were an ancient discovery. The ancient Greeks and Romans used what is known as lodestone, an iron-rich material, to attract other scraps of iron. The ancient Chinese even derived use from a magnet—they made magnetic compasses that they used for practicing a form of art, feng shui. These compasses were later used for navigation.

In the 13th century, Petrus Perigrinus, a French scholar, became one of the first people to study magnetism in detail and describe the properties of magnets. Afterward, William Gilbert, an English physician, analyzed the behaviour of magnets and was the first person to propose that the Earth behaved like a giant magnet. Over the next decades, more studies enabled a better understanding of what causes magnetism and its relation to electricity.

▶ Bar magnet

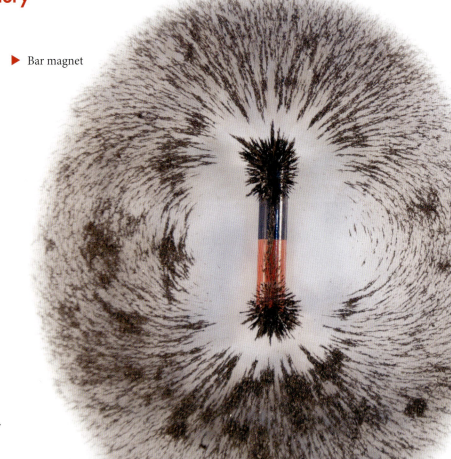

Properties of Magnets

Magnets always have two poles, a north pole (or a north-seeking pole) and a south pole (south-seeking pole).

The north pole attracts the south pole and repels the north pole of another magnet. In other words, like poles repel and unlike poles attract.

A magnet creates an invisible area of attraction or repulsion around it, which is known as its magnetic field.

The north pole of a magnet points towards the Earth's North Pole. This is because the Earth itself behaves like a giant magnet.

Cutting a magnet will not change its polarity of north and south poles. You'll merely get two magnets with their respective north and south poles.

Heating a magnet will make it lose some or all of its magnetic property.

Running a magnet over a magnetic material like an iron nail or a piece of nickel will convert that material into a magnet. This property is known as magnetisation.

FUN FACT
An MRI machine can produce a magnetic field about 60,000 times stronger than that of Earth!

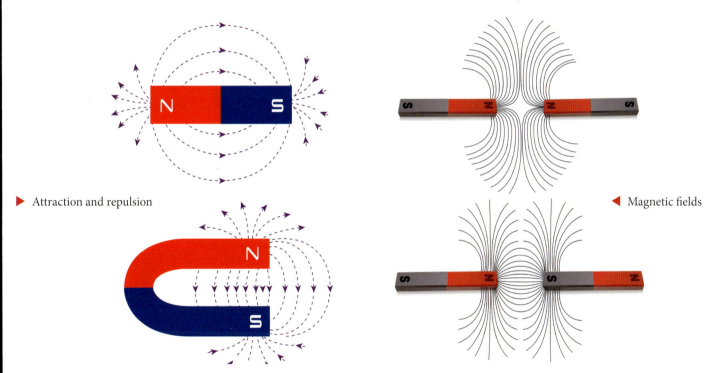

▶ Attraction and repulsion

◀ Magnetic fields

How Magnetism Works

Long before a detailed understanding of atoms and subatomic particles existed, the domain theory was used to explain magnetism. According to the theory, an iron bar (or any strong substance) contains many tiny pockets called domains. When the domains are arranged haphazardly, there is no magnetism. But when these domains are arranged in the same way, there is an overall magnetic field. When the iron bar is rubbed with a magnet, it becomes magnetised and all the domains that were originally haphazard are aligned so that they're pointing in the same way.

Later, it was discovered that the explanation for magnetism was inside the atoms that made up the magnetic material. More precisely, magnetism is the result of the rapid spinning of electrons. Since electrons are electrically charged particles, their motion resulted in magnetism. Each electron produced a tiny magnetic field. The sum total of the all these magnetic fields in a magnetic substance gives it its magnetic property.

Magnetic Field

The region surrounding a magnetic material or a moving electrical charge that can attract or repel other magnets or electric charges nearby is known as the material's magnetic field.

Earth as a Magnet

A magnetic compass's needle will point toward the north. While this phenomenon was known for many centuries, nobody knew the exact reason. It was in 1600 that an English scholar, William Gilbert, came up with an explanation.

When his work *De Magnete* was published, it was not only one of the first scientific books published in English, but also the first to describe Earth as a giant magnet. Later analysis did reveal that the Earth acted as a magnet, as it had many molten rocks rich in the magnetic material, iron. Like a bar magnet, the Earth's magnetic field stretches out into space. This region is known as the magnetosphere and extends for tens of thousands of kilometres beyond the ionosphere layer of Earth's atmosphere.

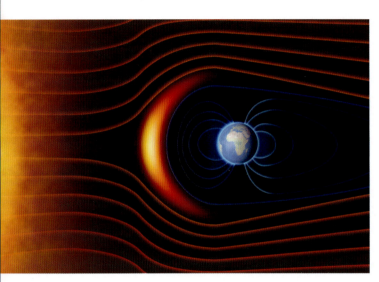

▲ Magnetosphere

The magnetosphere plays a crucial role in protecting the Earth from cosmic rays, ultraviolet radiation, and highly charged particles coming from the Sun and outer space, which would otherwise leach away Earth's upper atmosphere and ozone.

The Earth's magnetic field extends all the way from the planet's interior into space and is also known as the geomagnetic field. The field is created by electric currents caused by the motion of molten iron in the Earth's outer core and the escape of heat from the core.

The north and south magnetic poles of Earth, even though located near the geographic poles, tend to vary across geological time scales. Since the change occurs very slowly, magnetic compasses will remain accurate for navigation. Every few hundred thousand years, the Earth's magnetic field reverses completely.

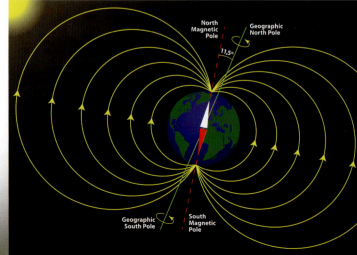

▲ Earth's magnetic field

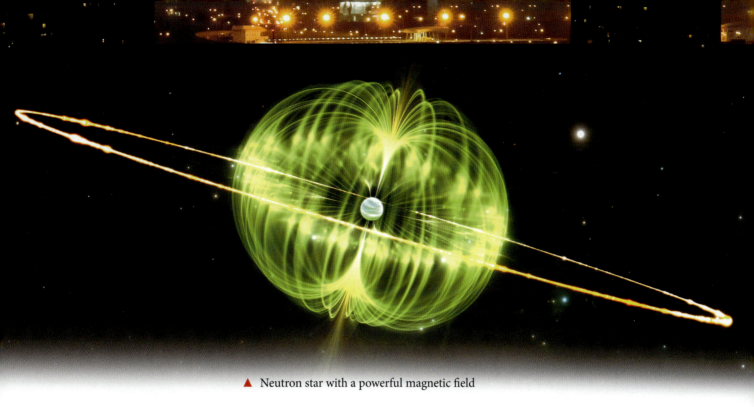

▲ Neutron star with a powerful magnetic field

Strength of Magnetic Field

A magnet's magnetic field strength is strongest close to the magnet and decreases with distance. The strength of the magnetic field is measured in units called teslas and gauss, named after two scientists.

Even though Earth is like a huge magnet, it has a surprisingly weak magnetic field. In fact, Earth's magnetic field is 100–1,000 times weaker than an average bar magnet. The biggest lab magnet on the planet exhibits a magnetic field that is 900,000 times stronger than that of Earth!

The Sun has a magnetic field many times stronger than the Earth's. Jupiter, Saturn, Uranus and Neptune also have magnetic fields stronger than that of Earth. However, Mercury, Venus and Mars have magnetic fields much weaker than Earth's. Our Moon does not exhibit any magnetism.

Neutron stars are small but dense and collapsed cores of large stars. They have the most powerful magnetic fields known in the universe, in the range of 104–1,011 teslas. To give a comparison, the highest magnetic field that has been generated in the laboratory is 16 teslas, enough to lift up a live frog.

FUN FACT

The northern lights (aurora borealis) and southern lights (aurora australis) are formed by charged particles in the solar wind interacting with Earth's magnetic field.

▼ Aurora borealis

Magnetic Materials

Magnets are not only interesting objects to play and experiment with; they are important components of appliances and technology we use every day. Different materials exhibit different degrees of magnetism.

▲ Magnets

▲ Neodymium magnets

Magnetic and Nonmagnetic Materials

When one thinks of magnets, iron is the first metal to come to mind. Iron exhibits strong magnetism. Other elements within the periodic table that also exhibit magnetism include some rare earth metals such as nickel, cobalt, samarium and neodymium.

Ferrites are compounds made of iron, oxygen and other elements and exhibit good magnetism. Lodestone, which is known as magnetite, is an example of a naturally occurring ferrite compound that was initially discovered and used by people in ancient times.

Other metals like copper, aluminium, gold and silver do not exhibit magnetism. Materials like wood, rubber, plastic, concrete, paper, glass, wool and cloth fibers do not exhibit magnetism either.

▲ Magnetic materials

Properties of Magnetic Materials

Even though iron is strongly magnetic, it is useful only as a temporary magnet, because it exhibits magnetism only when a magnet is brought near an iron object. Such a material is said to be 'magnetically soft.'

On the other hand, iron alloys and rare earth metals retain their magnetic properties even when they are removed from the magnetic field of another magnet. Such a material is said to be 'magnetically hard.' The extent to which a material can be magnetised is known as its 'susceptibility.'

Types of Magnetic Materials

▲ Steel bars

All known materials on Earth can be divided into one of three categories based on their magnetic properties: paramagnetic, ferromagnetic, and diamagnetic.

1) Paramagnetic: A material that, when hung from a thread, is capable of magnetising itself and aligning parallel to the Earth's magnetic field is said to be paramagnetic. Certain metals like aluminium and even many nonmetals are paramagnetic. The magnetism they exhibit is so weak that it is barely noticeable. Paramagnetic property is influenced by temperature—the hotter a paramagnetic material is, the less likely it is to respond to magnets placed close to it.

2) Ferromagnetic: Iron and a few other materials such as the rare earth metals become strongly magnetised in the presence of a magnetic field and have the ability to remain magnetised even after the magnetic field is removed. Such materials are said to be ferromagnetic. The word 'ferromagnetic' means 'magnetic like iron.' Ferromagnetic materials will lose their magnetism when they are heated above a certain temperature. This temperature is variable and known as the Curie temperature. For example, iron has a Curie temperature of 770°C, while nickel's Curie temperature is 800°C. Heating an iron magnet above its Curie temperature or repeatedly hitting it can weaken or destroy its ferromagnetic properties.

▲ Styrofoam is a diamagnetic material

3) Diamagnetic: While ferromagnetic and paramagnetic materials respond positively to magnetism, there are others that resist magnetisation. Such materials are said to be diamagnetic. Water and many carbon compounds are diamagnetic in nature. When a diamagnetic material is suspended on a string, it will align at an angle of 180 degrees to the Earth's magnetic field.

FUN FACT

Magnetically hard materials make good permanent magnets.

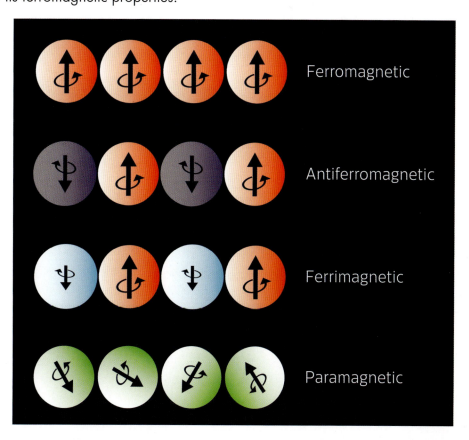

35

Magnetic Levitation

The use of magnetic fields to levitate or lift a mostly metallic object is known as magnetic levitation. In this process, the suspended object is supported only by magnetic fields. This technology is also sometimes referred to as 'electromagnetic suspension.'

Magnetic Levitation Principle

In magnetic levitation, electromagnetism is employed as a force to counteract gravity. However, levitation cannot be achieved by generating a simple electromagnetic field. A superconductor is used for making levitation viable and safe. A superconductor is a diamagnetic material that repels a magnetic field. This method of magnetic levitation is also known as 'electrodynamic propulsion.'

Maglev Trains

At present, with congested airports and frequent delays, people look for options other than flights to travel from one location to another. All other modes of transport apart from airplanes are too slow by today's standards. Scientists have devised a new and revolutionary alternative to air travel—maglev trains. A few countries have already developed high-speed maglev trains and operate them using powerful electromagnets.

Maglev (magnetic levitation) trains are designed to be suspended in air above the track and propelled forward to their destinations purely through magnetism. Since the trains are not directly in contact with the track, there is no friction except between the train carriages and the air. As a result, maglev trains can travel at very high speeds up to about 500 to 650 kilometres/hour. Better still, these trains can run at low noise levels and only consume relatively small amounts of energy.

◀ Maglev train

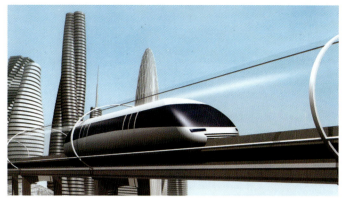

Maglev Trains and Conventional Trains

The maglev train differs considerably from a conventional train in more than one aspect. Maglev trains are not equipped with typical engines that are used for pulling carriages along the tracks. Maglev trains do not run on fossil fuels and instead are powered by the electrified coils of wire present in the track walls which propel them forward.

Maglev Train Operation

Maglev trains operate through three main components:

1) Large electrical power source

2) Metal coils lining a track

3) Large magnets attached to the underside of the train for guiding it along the track

FUN FACT
A maglev train typically floats on a cushion of air, levitating about 1 to 10 centimetres above the track.

The magnetised coils running along the track repel the large magnets present under the train.

Once the train is levitated, it receives power from the coils in the track walls to generate a system of magnetic fields to pull or push the train along the track.

The alternating current supplied to the coils is constantly altering so as to change the polarity of the magnetised coils. This change in polarity causes the magnetic field in front of the train to guide it forward.

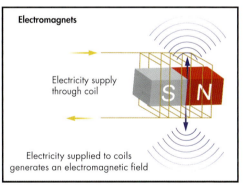
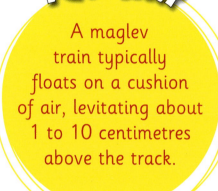
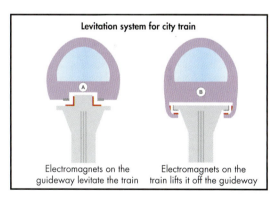
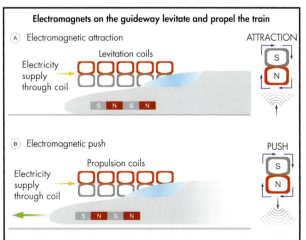
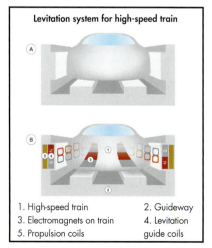

▲ Magnetic levitation mechanism

Electromagnetic Radiation

Electromagnetic (EM) radiation refers to a form of energy that we find everywhere around us. It can travel without any medium, unlike sound or vibrations, which need a medium for transmission. It is the energy emanated through the oscillation of a combination of electric and magnetic fields.

Discovery of EM Radiation

James Clerk Maxwell became the first scientist to suggest the existence of electromagnetic waves. He not only developed a scientific theory to describe EM radiation but also derived equations to describe the relation between the electric and magnetic fields. Maxwell's theory was later successfully applied to the generation of electromagnetic waves by another scientist, Heinrich Hertz.

▲ Electromagnetic wave

▲ James Clerk Maxwell

Properties of EM Radiation

Electromagnetic radiation is energy emitted radially through the combined vibrations of electrical and magnetic fields. Electromagnetic radiation has a dual nature—depending on the circumstances, it can act as a wave or particles. When EM radiation is treated as a wave, it will possess velocity, wavelength, and frequency. As particles, it is referred to as photons.

The electric and magnetic fields that make up an electromagnetic wave are perpendicular to each other along the direction in which it is travelling. EM radiation usually travels at the speed of light until it comes in contact with matter that can interfere with its propagation, such as a block of metal or water.

Generally, electromagnetic radiation is classified by wavelength into radio waves, microwaves, visible light (ranging from ultraviolet to the infrared range), X-rays and high-energy gamma rays.

The electromagnetic radiation classification is based on three main properties:

1) Energy: The energy of EM radiation is its intensity and is expressed in electron volts. Energy is calculated especially while measuring high-energy radiation like X-rays or gamma rays.

2) Wavelength: The wavelength of EM radiation is the measure of the distance between the wave repetitions. The wavelength is useful for describing the shape and movement of the wave.

3) Frequency: Frequency of an EM wave is the number of crests (maximum upward rise of a wave) and troughs (maximum downward point of a wave) passing through a point in any given second.

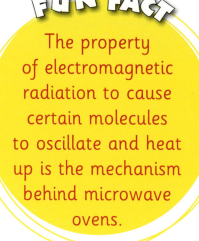

FUN FACT

The property of electromagnetic radiation to cause certain molecules to oscillate and heat up is the mechanism behind microwave ovens.

ELECTROMAGNETIC SPECTRUM

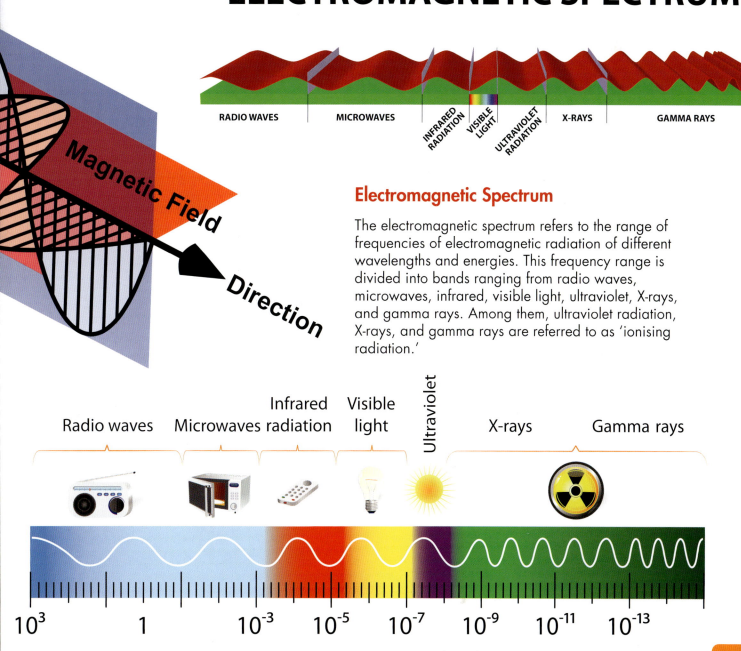

Electromagnetic Spectrum

The electromagnetic spectrum refers to the range of frequencies of electromagnetic radiation of different wavelengths and energies. This frequency range is divided into bands ranging from radio waves, microwaves, infrared, visible light, ultraviolet, X-rays, and gamma rays. Among them, ultraviolet radiation, X-rays, and gamma rays are referred to as 'ionising radiation.'

Electromagnetism

When the relationship between electricity and magnetism was identified, it led to a new branch of study and the development of many essential applications that we use every day in the modern world.

▶ Magnet and current generation in coil

Discovery of Electromagnetism

Hans Christian Oersted discovered the phenomenon of electromagnetism quite by accident in 1820 when he was in the midst of a lecture. He had suggested the possibility that electricity and magnetism could be related, but ended up proving it experimentally in front of his students. He passed electric current through a metallic wire and when a magnetic compass was suspended above it, the needle moved in response to the current.

Electromagnetic Properties

Electrons flowing through a conductor result in the formation of a magnetic field around the conducting material. The magnetic field lines will always be oriented perpendicularly to the direction of the flow of electricity.

The magnetic field produced by an electric wire can be increased by winding the wire into tight coils instead of stretching it out in a straight line. The magnetic field force produced by an electromagnet is called the magnetomotive force. This force is proportional to the product of current passing through the electromagnet and the number of coils in the wire.

The property of electromagnetism is extensively applied to many research, medical, industrial and daily purposes. One of the very first uses of an electromagnet was to power mechanical devices to produce mechanical force from electricity. The electric motor is the best example of one of the first applications of electromagnets.

▲ Electricity and magnetism relationship

Electromagnetic Induction

Just as the movement of electric current in a wire can generate a magnetic field, the movement of an electric wire through a magnetic field within a magnet will generate an electric current.

Fleming's left-hand rule is used for electric motors, while Fleming's right-hand rule is used for electric generators. We already have a magnetic field and motion of a wire through that field, so to calculate the direction of current induced, we use the right-hand rule.

With the three fingers of the right hand at right angles to each other, the thumb represents the direction of motion, the first finger the direction of the magnetic field, and the second finger the direction of the induced current.

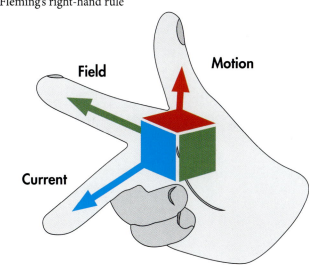

▶ Direction of current for generators, using Fleming's right-hand rule

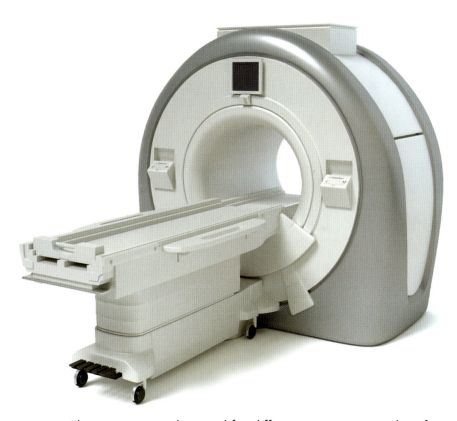

▶ An MRI machine uses a superconducting electromagnet.

An MRI is safer than X-ray or CT scans because it does not use harmful ionising radiation.

Electromagnets, designed for different purposes, can be of any of the three types:

1) Resistive: A resistive electromagnet uses copper wires or copper plates to generate magnetic fields. A magnetic field can be concentrated by twisting the wire around a piece of metal.

2) Superconducting: This type of electromagnet operates by reducing electrical resistance. It operates in very cold temperatures and can continue functioning even after the power supply is turned off.

3) Hybrid: This type of electromagnet is made by combining resistive and superconducting electromagnets.

Electromagnets

Today, scientists have identified that electromagnetism is one of the fundamental forces operating across the universe. It is responsible for electricity, magnetism and light. Starting with the demonstration of electromagnetism at the lab level, today it has become a regular feature in many devices and industrial processes we use.

▶ Hans Christian Oersted

History

Electromagnets came into existence following the breakthrough discovery by the Danish scientist Hans Christian Oersted. When a battery was turned on, the electric wire deflected the magnetic needle, leading him to propose that the electric wire radiated magnetic fields from all sides.

Oersted published his findings and mathematically proved that the current flowing through a wire produced a magnetic field. In 1824, about four years later, an English scientist, William Sturgeon, developed the first electromagnet.

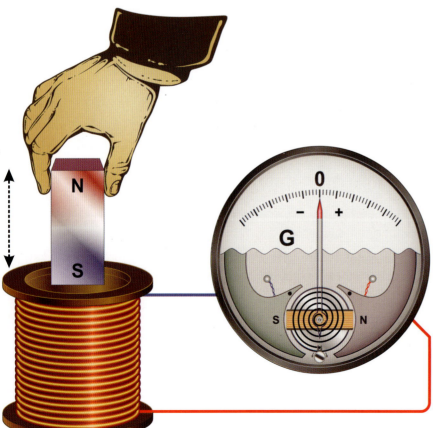

▲ Electric field in the presence of magnet

It was a horseshoe-shaped piece of iron wrapped tightly with copper wire. When current was passed through the wire, it attracted other pieces of iron scraps, but when the current supply was cut off, it lost its magnetisation property. By modern standards, the electromagnet designed by Sturgeon was too weak to be useful for any practical purpose. However, weighing about 200 grams, it was capable of lifting weights up to 9 pounds.

Later, in the 1930s, the American scientist Joseph Henry made many improvements in the basic design of the electromagnet to improve its efficiency. He used insulated wire and placed thousands of turns of wire on a single core. His electromagnet was so effective that it was capable of lifting and supporting weights of about 2000 lbs. Joseph Henry's revolutionary design modification made electromagnets popular and paved the way for innovations and uses for scientific, industrial, and practical purposes.

Working of an Electromagnet

An electromagnet is a piece of wire that is designed to generate a strong magnetic field when electric current is passed through it. All conducting materials and current-carrying wires generate a magnetic field, but an electromagnet is specially designed to maximise the strength of the magnetic field.

It is possible to construct a simple electromagnet at home by taking an iron nail and wrapping it tightly with copper wires in many coils and connecting the two ends to a battery. This 'electromagnet' is now capable of attracting small metal clips or iron filings.

Permanent Magnet versus Electromagnet

A permanent magnet has fixed north and south poles that cannot be altered or artificially fixed. In an electromagnet, the north and south polarity can be altered simply by changing the direction of electric current applied to a coil. A permanent magnet's magnetic field strength cannot be altered. An electromagnet's strength can be altered by changing the current flowing through the coil or by reducing or increasing the number of coils.

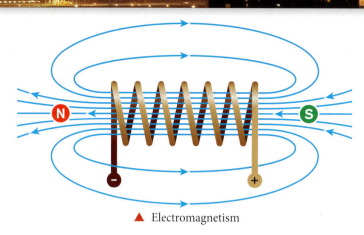
▲ Electromagnetism

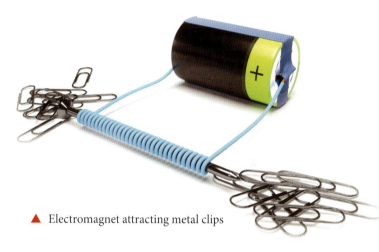
▲ Electromagnet attracting metal clips

▼ Electromagnet with many coils

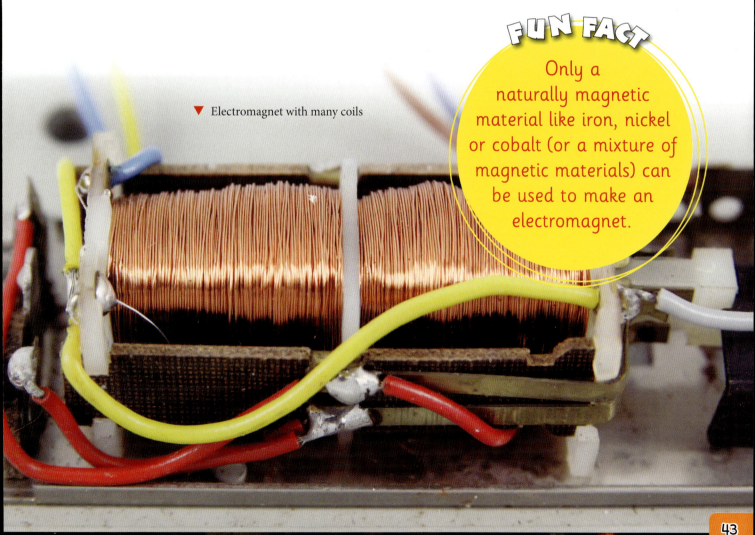

FUN FACT

Only a naturally magnetic material like iron, nickel or cobalt (or a mixture of magnetic materials) can be used to make an electromagnet.

Applications of Electromagnetism and EM Radiation

Electromagnetism and EM radiation serve many useful purposes. Today, many practical everyday applications as well as research depend largely on the direct or indirect employment of electromagnets or electromagnetic radiation.

▼ Large Hadron Collider

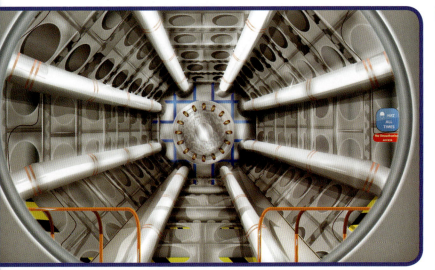

Uses of Electromagnetism

Ranging from minute electronic components to large-scale industrial machines, electromagnetism has many important applications. It is also used in research and experimentation purposes in many fields of science. Electromagnets offer an advantage over conventional magnets in that they can be controlled by switching the electricity on or off.

1. A solenoid is a type of electromagnet that is used in pinball machines, dot matrix printers, and paintball markers. All these devices require that magnetism be applied and controlled precisely for organised movement of certain components.

2. Superconducting electromagnets are used in scientific and research equipment such as nuclear magnetic resonance (NMR) spectrometers, mass spectrometers, and particle accelerators. The Large Hadron Collider (LHC) is an example of a massive particle accelerator.

3. Electromagnets are used in musical and sound equipment, including loudspeakers, earphones, and electric bells, and in magnetic recording and data storage in the form of tape recorders.

4. Electromagnets are also used in the multimedia and entertainment industry to create devices and components like data recorders and hard disks.

5. Electric actuators are motors used for converting electrical energy to mechanical energy, and use electromagnets to achieve this.

6. Power transformers function by increasing or decreasing voltage of alternating current transmitted along power lines. Electromagnetic induction is the principle behind the function of power transformation.

7. Induction cooking that uses electricity for heating and cooking food uses electromagnets.

8. Magnetic separators that sort and lift ferromagnetic material from scraps in the junkyard also use electromagnets.

9. MRI machines used for medical imaging and diagnosis employ electromagnets.

FUN FACT

The strength of electromagnets can also be controlled by increasing or decreasing the amount of electricity flowing around the electromagnet's core.

Uses of EM Radiation

EM radiation plays an important role in our everyday lives. Among the many applications, listed below are a few:

1. EM radiation in the form of long- and short-wavelength radio waves is used in broadcasting radio programs.

2. It is used widely in communication technology for transmitting TV, telephone, and wireless signals.

3. EM radiation is used in radars (radio sensing) for guiding and remote sensing for studying Earth's features.

4. Ultraviolet radiation is used in sterilization purposes for killing microbes and germs. It is also used for detecting forged paper currency.

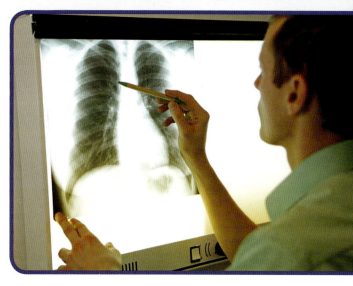

▲ Medical application of X-rays

5. X-rays can pass through the flesh and are used in detecting fractures or joint dislocations inside the body, and in general medical diagnosis.

6. Gamma rays are highly charged particles that can cause cancer upon exposure. However, they are also useful for killing cancer cells when used at the right levels.

7. Infrared radiation is used for night-vision devices and security cameras and is employed extensively by military forces across the world.

8. Microwaves are used for heating and cooking, employed in microwave oven technology. They are also used for satellite signals, as microwave radiation is capable of passing through clouds and atmosphere.

▲ Microwave oven

◀ Satellites capture radio wave signals.